W9-ARV-811

Moonscape:
The Surface of the Moon

By Mary Lindeen

Scott Foresman
is an imprint of

Glenview, Illinois • Boston, Massachusetts • Chandler, Arizona •
Upper Saddle River, New Jersey

Photographs

Every effort has been made to secure permission and provide appropriate credit for photographic material. The publisher deeply regrets any omission and pledges to correct errors called to its attention in subsequent editions.

Unless otherwise acknowledged, all photographs are the property of Pearson Education, Inc.

Photo locators denoted as follows: Top (T), Center (C), Bottom (B), Left (L), Right (R), Background (Bkgd)

Opener: PhotoLibrary Group, Ltd.
1 Michael Benson/Corbis
3 ©NASA Images/Alamy Images
4 Getty Images
5 Photolibrary Group, Ltd.
6 PhotoLibrary Group, Ltd.
7 Getty Images
8 ©Michael Benson/Corbis
9 PhotoLibrary Group, Ltd.
10 ©Bettmann/Corbis
11 Getty Images
12 Getty Images

ISBN 13: 978-0-328-46923-9
ISBN 10:   0-328-46923-8

Copyright © by Pearson Education, Inc., or its affiliates. All rights reserved. Printed in the United States of America. This publication is protected by copyright, and permission should be obtained from the publisher prior to any prohibited reproduction, storage in a retrieval system, or transmission in any form or by any means, electronic, mechanical, photocopying, recording, or likewise. For information regarding permissions, write to Pearson Curriculum Rights & Permissions, One Lake Street, Upper Saddle River, New Jersey 07458.

Pearson® is a trademark, in the U.S. and/or in other countries, of Pearson plc or its affiliates.
Scott Foresman® is a trademark, in the U.S. and/or in other countries, of Pearson Education, Inc., or its affiliates.

3 4 5 6 7 8 9 10 V010 13 12 11 10

Earth has one moon. It's much smaller than our planet. Before 1969, no humans had ever stepped on the moon.

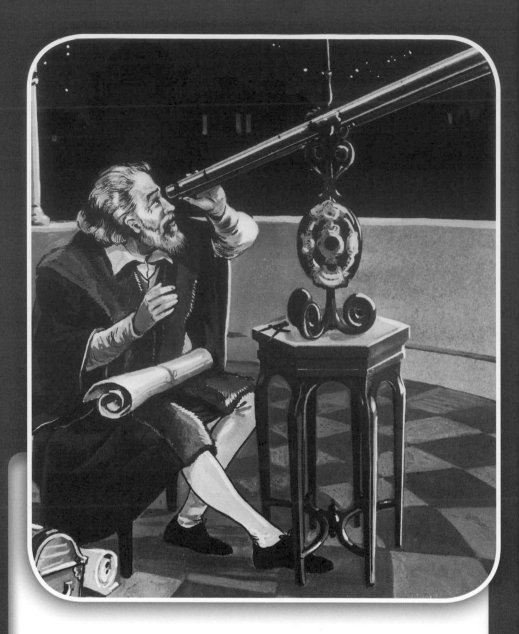

Humans have always wondered about the moon. Why is it in the sky? How does it change shape? What's it made of?

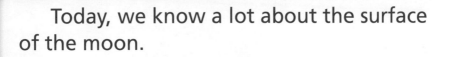

Today, we know a lot about the surface of the moon.

We know that the surface is very dry.
Most of it is crushed rock.

We know there is no wind on the moon. Nothing moves, not even a speck of dust. That's why these footprints are still on the surface. They were made more than 40 years ago.

There are two main areas on the moon's surface. They're called the seas and the highlands.

The seas aren't really seas at all. There is no water in them. The seas are thin layers of cooled lava. These areas look darker and smoother to us.

The far side of the moon is mostly highlands. They're made up of rocky surfaces. These areas look lighter and rougher to us.

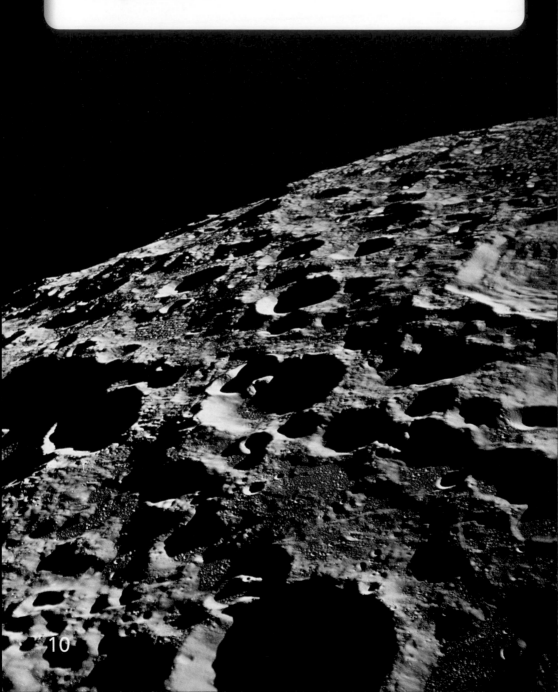

The moon's surface has many craters. Craters are bowl-like features made when asteroids and meteors hit the moon. Most of the craters are on the highlands.

The moon is closer to Earth than any planets or stars. But it isn't like Earth at all. There's no rain or wind. There's no air. Is there life on the moon? Not yet!